D0473412

To: Joy
Dec. 9/10, 1982

From: Helen D. Gunderson

On the occasion of:
blessings on your BD and
for the Christmas season
and your season of transition

FOR EVERYTHING THERE IS A SEASON

by Miriam Frost and Ned Skubic

Winston Press

Copyright © 1981 by Winston Press. All rights reserved.
Printed in the United States of America. 5 4 3 2
Library of Congress Catalog Card Number: 81-50550   ISBN: 0-86683-604-7
Winston Press, Inc.   430 Oak Grove   Minneapolis, MN 55403

For everything there is a season
and a time for every purpose
under heaven:

 time to be born,

and a time to die;

a time to plant and a time to uproot;

 time to kill,

and a time to heal;

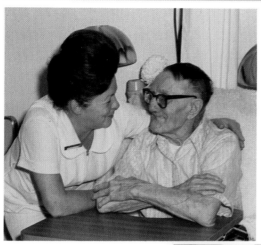

a time to break down
and a time to build;

 time to weep,

and a time to laugh;

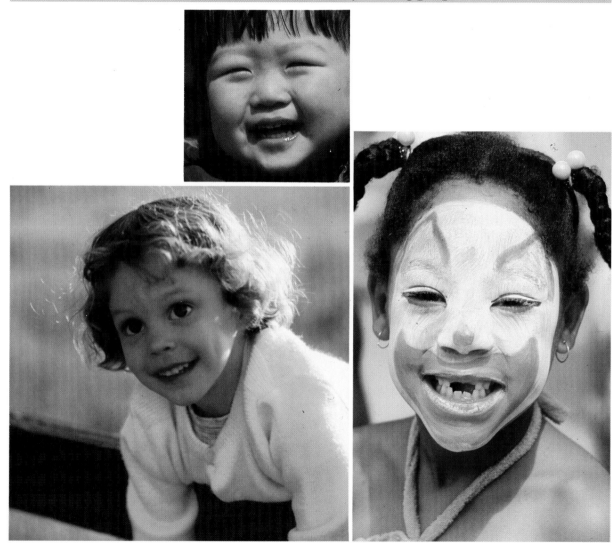

a time to mourn,

and a time to dance;

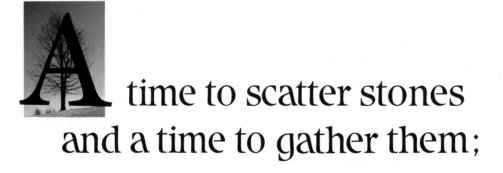 time to scatter stones
and a time to gather them;

a time to embrace
and a time to refrain from embracing;

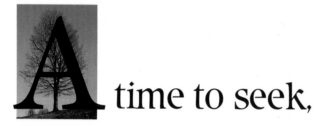 time to seek,

and a time to lose;

a time to keep
and a time to cast away;

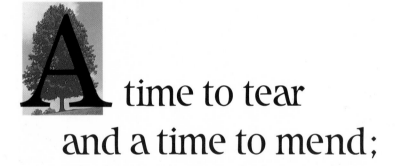 time to tear
and a time to mend;

a time to be silent
and a time to speak;

 time to love,

and a time to hate;

a time for war,

and a time for peace.

Photo Credits

Peter G. Aitken — 7, bottom right; 16

Ken Bazyn — 23

Cheryl Walsh Bellville — 12, top left; 13, bottom right; 15; 19; 42; 52; 53, top left; 57, right

Jim Bradshaw — 40

Dennis E. Cox — 20, left; 48, foreground

Robert J. Cunningham — 56-57, background

Joseph A. DiChello, Jr. — 9; 21, left; 27, top; 35, background; 41; 43, foreground

Randy Dieter/Corn's Photo Service — 55

Robert M. Friedman — cover; ii; initial capitals; 5; 6; 7, top right; 12-13 spread; 20-21, background; 33, bottom; 45; 47; 50; 51; 56, right; 64

Vivienne della Grotta — 39

Stewart M. Green/Tom Stack & Associates — 38-39

Michael Hayman/Corn's Photo Service — 21, right

John Maines — 10

Tom Mcguire — 11; 27, bottom left

Paul Robert Perry, Ltd — 26

Cyril A. Reilly — 17; 20, right; 35, foreground; 57, left; 59

Mark W. Schwartz — 18

Jackie Sheckler — 30

John Sheckler — 27, bottom right; 31; 37; 61, background; 63

Ned Skubic — i; 8; 25, background; 28; 33, top; 43, background; 48-49, background; 49, foreground; 53, bottom right; 60; 62

Rick Smolan — 24; 29; 44

Dick Sroda/Corn's Photo Service — 61, foreground

Bob Taylor — 25, foreground

Vivian M. Turcott — 56, left